D0772650

Ronaldinho

José María Obregón

English translation: Megan Benson

PowerKiDS press™

Editorial Buenas Letras™
New York

Published in 2008 by The Rosen Publishing Group, Inc.
29 East 21st Street, New York, NY 10010

First Edition
Book Design: Nelson Sa

Cataloging Data

Obregón, José María, 1967-
   Ronaldinho / Arturo Contró; English translation: Megan Benson — 1st ed.
p.cm. – (World Soccer Stars / Estrellas del fútbol mundial)
   Includes Index.
   ISBN: 978-1-4042-7664-2
   1. Ronaldinho–Juvenile literature. 2. Soccer players–Biography–Juvenile literature.
3. Spanish-language materials.

Manufactured in the United States of America

Photo Credits: Cover (left) © Luis Gene/Getty Images; cover (right) © Alex Livesey/Getty Images; p. 5 © Kamal Moghrabi/Getty Images; p. 7 © Pedro Armestre/Getty Images; p. 7 (inset) © www.youtube.com; p. 9 © Antonio Scorza/Getty Images; p. 11 © Jean-Philippe Ksiazek/Getty Images; p. 13 © Clive Mason/Getty Images; p. 15 © Bagu Blanco/Getty Images; p. 17 © Franck Fife/Getty Images; p. 19 © Cesar Rangel/Getty Images; p. 21 © Jefferson Bernardes/Getty Images.

Contents

Contenido

Ronaldo de Assis Moreira is a Brazilian soccer player known as Ronaldinho. Ronaldinho means "Little Ronaldo." Ronaldinho was born on March 21, 1980, in Porto Alegre, Brazil.

Ronaldo de Assis Moreira es un futbolista brasileño conocido como Ronaldinho, que quiere decir "pequeño Ronaldo". Ronaldinho nació el 21 de marzo de 1980, en la ciudad de Porto Alegre, Brasil.

Ronaldinho has been good at soccer since he was very young. When he was 13, he **scored** 23 goals in a single game!

Desde pequeño, Ronaldinho demostró ser muy bueno para el fútbol. A los trece años de edad, ¡Ronaldinho **anotó** 23 goles en un solo partido!

In 1997, Ronaldinho helped the Brazilian team win the U-17 **World Cup**. This is the World Cup for players younger than 17.

En 1997, Ronaldinho ayudó a la selección de Brasil a ganar el Mundial sub-17. Esta es la **Copa del Mundo** para jugadores menores de 17 años.

Ronaldinho

Ronaldinho's first professional team was the Gremio de Porto Alegre, in Brazil. In 2001, Ronaldinho went to play for a team in **Europe**, the Paris Saint-Germain, in France.

El primer equipo de Ronaldinho fue el Gremio de Porto Alegre de Brasil. En 2001, Ronaldinho fue a jugar a un equipo de **Europa**, el Paris Saint-Germain, en Francia.

With Brazil, Ronaldinho won the 2002 World Cup. Ronaldinho surprised soccer fans with his great skills and speed.

Ronaldinho ganó con Brasil la Copa del Mundo 2002. Ronaldinho causó gran admiración entre los espectadores por su pericia y velocidad para jugar con el balón.

In 2003, Ronaldinho joined
FC Barcelona, in Spain. Ronaldinho
helped Barcelona win the European
Champions League in 2006.

En 2003, Ronaldinho pasó al FC
Barcelona de España. Ronaldinho
ayudó al Barcelona a ganar la Liga
de Campeones de Europa, en 2006.

Ronaldinho has won the FIFA Best World Player Award twice, in 2004 and in 2005. He also won the Golden Ball in 2005. This award is given to the best player in Europe.

Ronaldinho ha ganado el premio FIFA como mejor jugador del mundo dos veces, en 2004 y 2005. Además, ganó el premio Balón de Oro, en 2005. Este premio se le da al mejor jugador de Europa.

Ronaldinho is not just a great soccer player. He enjoys playing every game. Ronaldinho always plays with a big smile.

Ronaldinho no sólo es un gran jugador de fútbol. Ronaldinho disfruta mucho de cada partido. Ronaldinho siempre juega con una gran sonrisa.

Ronaldinho enjoys spending time with his family. His **idols** are his parents, Joao de Silva and Miguelina, and his brothers, Roberto, and Deisi.

Ronaldinho disfruta mucho de su familia. Entre sus grandes **ídolos** están sus padres, Joao de Silva y Miguelina, y sus hermanos, Roberto y Deisi.

Glossary / Glosario

Europe (**yur**-up) The continent where countries like Spain and France are located.

idols (**eye**-duhlz) People that you love or admire very much.

scored (**skord**) Made a point or points in a game.

World Cup (**wur**-uld **kup**) A soccer tournament that takes place every four years with teams from around the world.

---

anotar Conseguir uno o varios goles.

Copa del Mundo (la) Competencia de fútbol, cada cuatro años, en la que juegan los mejores equipos del mundo.

Europa El continente donde se encuentran Francia, España y otros países.

ídolos (los) Personas por las que se siente mucho amor o admiración.

Resources / Recursos

Books in English/Libros en inglés

Shea, Therese. Soccer Stars. Danbury, CT: Children's Press, 2007

Books in Spanish/Libros en español

Page, Jason. El fútbol. Minneapolis: Two-Can Publishers, 2001

Web Sites

Due to the changing nature of Internet links, The Rosen Publishing Group has developed an online list of Web sites related to the subject of this book. This site is updated regularly. Please use this link to access the list:

www.buenasletraslinks.com/ss/ronaldinho

Index

Índice